Survival Kit
for Writers Who
Don't Write Right

Nonfiction by Patricia McLinn

Word Watch: A Writer's Guide to the Slippery, Sneaky and Otherwise Tricky

"*Word Watch* does for the common man or woman what Theodore Bernstein's *The Careful Writer* does for the scholarly intellectual. Far more extensive than Bernstein, having been created over the course of years, it's a valuable reference and a good read rolled into one."

—*5-star review*

"Keep it handy on your desk. Take it along for casual browsing … Read four or five entries a day to give your brain a good workout—and your spirit a good laugh."

—*5-star review*

Survival Kit

for Writers Who

Don't Write Right

Patricia McLinn

Can you survive in publishing genre fiction if you don't outline, if you go AWOL from character interviews, if you go cross-eyed at color-keyed plot charts, and if you would rather clean a sewer than write a synopsis?

Whether you're indie, traditional, or hybrid, the answer is yes. A veteran bestselling author shares how she's survived and thrived through 50 books and 30 years in publishing.

USA Today bestselling author Patricia McLinn, who has taught writing from Australia to Washington, D.C., presents practical, proven, and hard-won tips and tools for those who don't write "right."

Contents

Introduction

Patricia McLinn

Welcome!

This is going to be part revival meeting, part workshop-in-a-book. So, get comfortable.

A lot of us who are pantsers* or extreme pantsers are used to being considered writers who don't write right. However, there are writers who are considered not writing "right" for other reasons and they're welcome here, too.

(*What's a pantser? Someone who writes without plotting out the story ahead of time. People who do plot out the story ahead of time are—not surprisingly—called plotters.)

Before we start, I want to share my top two tips about writing and a statement (some might say a warning) about this book.

Number One Writing Tip:
All writing advice is a buffet. Not a fixed menu.

That means you're in charge of what you try, what you skip, how much you take, if you go back for seconds, or if you give something a shot this time that you passed up last time.

Number Two Writing Tip:
No other writer can tell you what will work for you. They can only tell you what's worked for them.

You are the only one living inside your writing process (or having it live inside of you, depending on how you look at it.)

So, consider all that advice displayed on the buffet and remember it's your process that will taste and digest the healthy stuff and the goodies. Doesn't matter if it works for 98 percent of other writers if it leaves your process queasy.

Statement/Warning:
This book does not offer a recipe for a method—surefire or otherwise. It offers tips and tools I hope you can try applying to your individual process as it grows, adapts, and sharpens.

It's a short book by design.

I don't want to waste your time.

It seldom slows down for explanations. It's for writers with some words under their belts. It might be helpful to those just starting out, but they might need to find definitions of terminology. Feel free to contact me if I've lost you.

It is not a pantser vs. plotter book.

It does **not** say don't plot. Anyone who thinks that needs to read it a second time more carefully. Or read it for the first time before making such statements.

It also doesn't say to plot.

It says to do what works for you.

Then it offers tips and tools for writers who are pantsing or otherwise not writing "right."

If you're really short on time, skip Part I. It's about how I came to compile my Survival Kit and share it with you.

PART I

Why Writers Who Don't Write Right
Need a Survival Kit

There's a moment in the old movie *Holiday* when Cary Grant turns to Katharine Hepburn and says, "There's a conspiracy against us, child."

I know just how he felt. If you do, too, there's a chance you don't write "right."

Years ago, I was on a book tour of Louisiana and Texas with an RV full of fellow authors. It was always exhausting, usually fun, highly educational, and altogether an adventure. That trip's definitely worth a book someday. (Might need to be written by the last survivor of the group to avoid lawsuits. Kidding. ... Mostly.)

At one stop, we talked to a writing class at a community college near Houston.

The teacher, who was sitting next to me at one end of the panel, asked us to each tell the class how we wrote—our methods and routines—and started at the far end of the panel. Coming down the line, we heard about detailed outlines, writing a set number of pages or words each day, writing at the same time every day, precise color-coded charts, filled-out software questionnaires, novels written exactly to length with no trimming or adding necessary.

Then, as the last one, it was my turn.

I told them I don't outline. Wouldn't write a synopsis if I didn't have to. (This was in my traditionally published era, so I did have to.) When I start a book, I know bits and pieces of the story (never the whole thing) and odd elements of the characters, but must write the book to find out what my story is. I riddle manuscripts with notes set off by brackets. I also use brackets to ask myself questions, such as [Why on earth is he doing this???? Must have a reason!]

I have no set schedule. Binge on writing one day, then might go two or three without writing anything. I invariably think I'm coming in shorter than usual, but instead write long and have to cut, which to my mind makes the book stronger. I have an office and a desk, but move around the house to write, sometimes several times in one writing session.

I'll start without character names, calling them he, she, xxx, abc, efg, or The Neighbor until I know the right name. If there's a natural chapter or scene break I indicate it, but I don't do the final chapter and scene breaks until the manuscript is complete.

I write what I know when I know it.

That means I've started a number of books by writing a scene from the middle. I might know it will end up somewhere in the middle when I write it, but that's what came to me first.

And sometimes I start writing the scene from its middle. Or its end.

Then I jump to the next thing I know.

All of which means I mostly write out of sequence. And that means I need to fill in and smooth. A lot.

When I finished, the writing teacher closed her gaping mouth, turned from me to her class, and said, "Don't do that. Ever."

At that time I'd published more than a dozen books. Yet she had a point.

At least part of a point.

Good? Bad? Definitely Old Days

When I started writing and submitting fiction, it was under the system now called traditional publishing, or trad. Back then it was just publishing.

The way it was supposed to work was that the author came up with a dynamite and "hooky" concept, wrote the first three chapters and a synopsis of the entire book, sent it to his/her agent, who loved, loved, loved it and sent it to the perfect editor for that book, then immediately called the author with encouraging and praiseful words.

The editor loved, loved, loved it and immediately bought the book, giving the author both an advance on royalties that would support the author during the time the book was being written and a reasonable deadline. The editor put through the first part of the advance so the author received it even before said author could wonder when it would arrive.

While the author worked steadily and sanely on the book—while also continuing to have a life that included regular exercise, reasonable eating habits, healthy relationships, and unstrained eyes—the editor lined up a cover that accurately represented the book and would grab prospective readers' attention, as well as planning and implementing marketing to widen that pool of prospective readers to its maximum potential.

The author would turn in a book that sustained, nay, exceeded, the promise of the first three chapters. The editor loved, loved, loved the completed manuscript and put through payment of that portion of the advance immediately. The line edit made only a dozen changes, each of which strengthened the book immeasurably, the copyedit corrected four typos and one tiny factual error, the proofread caught two typos the copyedit missed. The author read the page proofs/ author pages with joy and delight, making precisely one change of one word that turned that sentence, paragraph, chapter, book from wonderful to orgasmic.

The check for the "acceptance" portion of the advance was put through instantly and the book slotted for near-immediate release as a lead title that the publishers' marketing team enthusiastically and effectively sold to bookstores that employed only book-loving super-salespeople who worked tirelessly to match reader and book.

The End.

You did notice that I write fiction for a living, didn't you?

Because it didn't actually work that way. Not the business side and not the creative side. For some of us the reality was far beyond any terrors Tim Burton and Stephen King combined could imagine.

Yet that teacher at that community college truly did have part of a point.

Because the proposal—the first three chapters and a synopsis of the entire book—was the cornerstone of the business at that time.

Things have changed over the years.

For those authors who now choose to be independent—selling to readers through vendors such as Kindle, Apple Books, Kobo, Nook, and more—rather than through traditional publishing, the first three chapters and synopsis are not necessary. (I'd sing the Hallelujah Chorus if it wouldn't break your ears.)

In traditional publishing, it's gone from difficult to nearly impossible for first-time authors to sell on proposal.

First-time and, in many instances, established authors need to submit a completed manuscript, often accompanied by information about their marketing plans—self-funded—and their personal "platform." Whether an established author can sell on proposal will depend on his/her most recent publishing history, the story idea, relationship with the editor/publisher, and the general approach of the publishing house.

But back when we talked to that Texas writing class and for years afterward, I always told authors that if they could possibly write by outlining and starting at the beginning then writing straight through, they should. Because that meshed with the biz.

In contrast, my non-method process had the darnedest time cramming its irregular shape into the precisely square hole of traditional publishing's requirements.

I frequently did the first draft of an entire book before I could write a synopsis, wiping out any benefit of selling on a proposal. Plus, not only was the finished book usually quite different from my synopsis—

(That happens a lot, including to authors who outline, which might make you wonder why a synopsis is required, and I'm right there with you in the wondering. The reason given was always "marketing." In my career that was always unicorn marketing. Heard it existed, never saw it.)

—but often the first three chapters I'd sent in didn't much resemble the first three chapters in the final book.

But, I told the students in that Houston area writing class and many others when the publishing world still toiled solely under the trad model, **if the choice is to write your weird way or not write at all, then there is no choice.**

Get on with writing weird.

If other methods produce fewer—or zero—words on the page/screen, there is no chance at all of having a writing career.

I am proof you could keep your creativity cooking and still survive in the biz as it was then. I published 27 books in 25 years with trad publishers.

And, you know what? As I described my decidedly non-methodical process, I saw a number of faces brighten in that writing class audience. Several came up to me afterward, thanking me for the encouragement because that's how they wrote. I'd given them hope.

Granted, they told me that when the teacher wasn't listening ... which seemed wise.

Beginning of a Quest

That sparked my years-long effort to offer a Survival Kit for Writers Who Don't Write Right workshop at writers' conferences. By that point, I'd attended a whole lot of workshops and conferences myself and had yet to see anything for those of us who don't write "right."

That dearth continued. Organizers gladly signed me up to give workshops on characterization, dialogue, editing, or dealing with the media, but turned down Survival Kit without a moment's hesitation.

Eventually, I theorized that people who organize conferences (and to whom we all owe great gratitude for those efforts!) have a different mindset from those of us who don't write "right." Perhaps they need that different mindset to organize conferences. They genuinely cannot fathom that this could work for anybody, so why waste a program slot for it?

Then, around 2001, fellow author Alicia Rasley gave me the opportunity to present the Survival Kit workshop at a national Romance

Writers of America conference in New York. Alicia not only was the program chair that year, she also was a teacher and had encountered other writers who write the way I do. At least somewhat.

Reasonably, the session was scheduled for a tough timeslot and in a small room. I figured I might be the only one in attendance.

That day I was more nervous about giving a workshop than before or since. When the first few people came into the room, I told them if it was just us, we'd go to the bar and I'd give the presentation there.

But more and more people arrived, reaching respectable status, then beyond ... I stopped looking at that point because I didn't want my nobody's-coming nerves to flip over to omg-how-many-people-am-I-talking-to? nerves.

After I gave that earliest version of the workshop that spawned this book, writers—both aspiring and published—came up to the front with tears in their eyes, saying they never knew anyone else wrote that way.

I told them to look around.

You are not alone.

The same thing happened at the Romance Writers of Australia conference in 2015 in Melbourne when I gave the Survival Kit workshop. (Love the iconoclast Aussies, who didn't hesitate over having me do this workshop. Great conference, great people.)

A crowd that warmed my heart included many with teary eyes when I pointed out they were not alone in not writing "right."

One attendee stopped me in the hall later in the day and said she'd decided before the conference that it would be her last, that she was going to give up writing because she couldn't do it the way the how-to books said she needed to. But after Survival Kit she'd decided to continue giving it a go. I heard from her almost a year later and she'd completed her first book.

More and more of us not-right writers are slowly opening up to tell our stories. And finding platforms where we can.

We're no longer anonymous. You're no longer alone.

It can be done.

It is done.

You can do it.

On to Part II, which looks at the big picture of living your process and tips on experimenting. It also includes wise words (if I do say so myself) that put the tools and tips that will follow into context.

PART II

First Item in Your Survival Kit:
A Teeter-Totter

Up. Writers need to respect and nurture their individual process of getting words down on the page/up on the screen.

Down. At the same time, they benefit from being open to exploring and experimenting with new-to-them methods and approaches.

Up. You never know when you're going to find something that makes your writing richer, easier, faster, deeper. You sure don't want to miss those opportunities by rigidly refusing to consider any other method.

Down. On the other hand, writers who don't write right are going to need to withstand a whole lot of urging to disrespect their own processes, to jettison them immediately and completely for the one, the only, the true Right

Way to Write. (There are many of these "one and onlys.")

If you're really good at balance, you can find that perfect spot in between the ups and downs, and teeter there for a long time.

Otherwise, you'll pass through that sweet spot briefly as you're coming or going—grab those moments, appreciate them, do your best to extend them. And recognize that the ups and downs are as temporary as the sweet spot.

Pressure to Write Right

The writing world equivalent of "What's your sign?" is "Are you a plotter or a pantser?"

Plotter, in case you missed it in Part I, is a writer who plots out (often by way of an outline) his or her book before starting to write.

I also think of plotters as builders of stories. They know what form the story will take and they begin at the bottom and construct it.

Pantser—as in one who flies by the seat of one's pants—is a writer who begins writing without a flight plan or a map. Author Jo Beverly referred to it as "flying into the mists."

The pantsers I've met are discovery writers. We have an idea and we start writing it, seeing where that idea takes us and what it creates.

Neither method is superior to the other. It comes from how the author's mind works and, sometimes, from the needs of the individual book.

There are lots and lots and lots of books (as well as workshops) out there about writing fiction as a plotter. Their titles count the steps, the days, the elements that will carry you to a perfect book. Some tell you to drop—or set fire to—your pants, others threaten that you'll die if you don't plot, many stress plotting is the only way to sell books.

I'm not making any guarantees about or to you, but I'm standing here as proof—I haven't died, I have sold books, and I am a writer who doesn't write "right."

My first book was sold to traditional publisher Harlequin in 1989 and came out in 1990. It was the first book I'd ever submitted. (Don't worry, I had plenty of rejections later.) In the early years I continued to work full-time, later part-time as an editor for the Washington Post, which certainly cut into my writing time. (Darned day jobs ... which, for me, was mostly an afternoon-night job.) After 23 years at the Post, I left in 2007 to write full-time.

I trad published 27 books in 25 years. I started indie publishing in 2010, remaining a hybrid author by publishing with a traditional publisher until 2015, when I became fully indie.

As an indie, I've been on the USA Today bestseller list multiple times. (At least six; I really should go look it up.) Indie has also been lucrative for me. Nowhere near the level of a number of authors who've had phenomenal success. (Those who persisted after being told by traditional publishing that they'd never succeed particularly warm my heart.) I am making a good living writing books I love—around 50 titles so far.

And yet, I get the pressure. Both external and internal.

Yes, internal.

When I decided to try my hand at mysteries, I told myself my process worked okay for romances, even women's fiction. But with a mystery, surely I had to plot.

So I tried.

Two and a half years later, no mystery. (I wrote romances in the interim, using my process.)

The light bulb goes off.

Gee, maybe I could try a mystery writing my way.

Seven years later, I've published ten of them, working on the eleventh as I write this. (Along with continuing to write romances.)

But I'm not the only one who told me I had to plot.

Having survived in the biz, having good things happen, especially as an indie, I still hear from other authors and writing gurus in person, on forums, or by email an average of a dozen times a year that I really should outline. That I'll be more productive, earn more money, write more easily if I totally change the way I write.

You will hear these things, too.

The vast majority of the advice and promises will be well-meant.

The really tricky part is that—for some of you—the promises might be true.

Plotting Math

Tip: Before assessing the claims, beware the plotting proselytizers' math.

Frequently, they rave about how much faster they write with an outline. They might ask you how many words you wrote in three hours, say, and their total will come out way ahead.

Hah!

They're not counting the thinking and creating time of producing the outline. Word count-per-hour is not an informative comparison unless they add that in.

Plotters segment their time into plotting/outlining/thinking and writing, with word-count-per-hour covering only the writing part of their process.

For pantsers, the writing and thinking are braided together, so our thinking time is baked into our word count-per-hour.

Is it possible a plotter is faster than you even if they count in the plotting/outlining/thinking time? Sure. But make them do all the math before claiming speed benefits from plotting.

Stupidly Stubborn vs. Profligately Pliable

I advocate protecting and respecting your process.

But.

In fact, **BUT**.

Don't close yourself off to other possibilities.

Tip: If you dismiss outlining or other plotting methods without assessing them, you could be missing out. I encourage each of you to experiment, but with some precautions.

I've tried outlining. Three and a half times.

The first two times I totally lost the stories I was trying to outline.

What do I mean by "lost" them?

They were written down in outline form, but now, many years later, they have never become books. Best I can tell, my brain considers them done. Story's told. All complete. Let's go find something new to play with.

Each time I've tried to write from those outlines—and I have tried—my brain/creativity/muse has gone into full rebellion. Bored. Bored. Bored. Will not come out to play.

So, did I give up on outlining?

Hah!

I tried again when Scrivener hit the broad audience. Everyone—literally everyone—was saying it was the best thing ever and they had no idea how they'd written without it. As someone who could not have written one, much less 50 books without cut and paste, Scrivener seemed like it should be ideal for me. Scrivener, here I come!

I transferred a three-quarters complete manuscript that I wanted to work on into Scrivener, planning to move pieces around into an outline to help me reshape the manuscript.

Did not work for me.

It felt as if the book had become a disjointed archipelago with isolated islands, none of which was a piece of the whole story as I felt it.

(This did not end up as a lost story. I pulled it all back into much-maligned Microsoft Word, reorganized it without outlining, cut about 40,000 words, wrote about 60,000 new words and published it in 2018 as the romantic mystery **Proof of Innocence**.)

Not one to give up easily, I tried a new idea in Scrivener, too. It dribbled into short, uninspired, unconnected drips and drabs. I couldn't get any sense for the wholeness of the story. I couldn't see or hear its rhythm. … And if that all sounds weird to you, insert your own terminology for how you interact with your stories.

(Also, I spent far too much time accumulating research I never used into Scrivener. Procrastination at its worst. It became the looks-like-I'm-working equivalent of online solitaire.)

I started a new new story back in my old standby of Word and wrote it at my usual pace (sloooow, sloooow, sloooow, panic fast, edit the bejeezus out of it, panic fast filling in, more editing, more editing, realize I'm putting back in words I'd previously removed, finally quit), liked it, and published it. That told me that I hadn't suddenly lost my ability to write.

Eventually, I transferred those dribs and drabs of the new effort started on Scrivener to Word. They became a Wyoming Wildflowers series romance, **Jack's Heart,** using my usual method.

The first two outline efforts still lie flat and dead in their files in my computer. Each time I open one of those files and try to work up interest, my muse demands a nap instead.

(Cautiously) Experiment With Outlining

Despite these experiences, I do recommend experimenting, including with outlining.

While we should respect and honor our process, it's a danger, in my opinion, to let ourselves become precious about when and how we write.

So, respect and honor, but push the edges now and then. We can all learn stuff.

I do have suggestions/cautions.

Tips on Experimenting

Tip: Something as widely written about as plotting or outlining produces piles of potential methods. You need to sort through them, rejecting all that don't click for you. There are so many possibilities, why waste any time on those that don't appeal? Life's too short. Writing time's too precious.

Tip: Beware of methods that guarantee results, then say if it doesn't work it's because you did it wrong. It's using snake oil sales tactics by making any failure the fault of the consumer.

Tip: Don't try new methods when you're on deadline.

Tip: Don't experiment with a story that's particularly dear to you in case you "lose" it.

Tip: On the flip side, a problem project is not a fair experiment. If it didn't work with your usual approach and it doesn't work with your experimental approach, you can't blame the experimental approach.

Tip: Proceed with caution. Test the waters carefully so a project doesn't drown.

For example, if you can feel a method you're trying stifling your creativity, then stop. If the writing grinds to a halt, then stop. Re-start that project with your usual process. If it stays stuck, it might have nothing to do with method. If it takes off with your usual process, then that's evidence the experimental approach might not work for you.

Try outlining a different project. If it gets stuck in the same spot, maybe the issue is not the method, but that spot.

Not Outlining Is Not Irrational

Sometimes the pressure to write "right" is not quite as direct as the threatening/promising titles of some how-to books.

I recall discussing this with one conference organizer who'd known me for a while. After I explained the premise of Survival Kit, she said with a pained expression, "But you're so rational about other things."

Well, yeah, I am.

I'm proud of my career as a journalist, including those 23 years as an editor at the Washington

Post. I'm also proud of being a past-president of Novelists, Inc., the international organization of multi-published popular fiction authors. Those are among the responsible positions I've success-fully held. Now I run my own publishing business, including contributing to the employ-ment of numerous other people. I also successfully handle personal finances, buying and selling houses, cross-country moves, international travel, and other elements of being a fully functioning adult. I like to think "a good head on her shoulders" applies.

I just happen to not be a linear thinker when I'm writing. That's not irrational.

Ah, but there is a major catch to not writing "right."

The Catch—You Knew There Had to Be One

It's one of the reasons the workshops and how-to books on specific methods abound, while there are not a lot of workshops or books about pantsing and otherwise not writing right.

As I said up front, this Survival Kit does not include **THE Answer**—and let's face it, isn't that what we all want? It sure would be easier.

THE Answer is what too many of those workshops and how-to books promise—sometimes explicitly. Follow these specific steps, work precisely this many days, cover those essential elements, and voila! you have a publishable book.

The truth is, there is no solitary answer, no single secret to writing a book. There's the intersection of your individual approach and a story idea. Then there's hard work and persistence, rinse and repeat. Over and over and over.

But here's the flip side of that. Even if there were a singular Answer, a Secret, it wouldn't be Magic—at least not for me—and not for you if you're still reading this.

Remember the builders and discoverers?

Some writers build a story. In fact, a lot of how-tos use that terminology, with references to foundations and beams and such.

I don't build a story as much as discover it.

At the start of a story, for me it's like seeing a landscape in patches through Jo Beverly's mists.

Some of those patches are absolutely clear and certain. Often those are small, seemingly trivial details—details that far more often than not end up being important. I just didn't see their importance until those particular mists cleared.

Surrounding the initial clear patches are swaths of unknown. It's my job to explore the unknown. And to reveal it.

That's the basis of my process.

Pushing into those mists, exploring them, while also staying within the boundaries of reader expectations.

Tip: Reader Expectations—When you write genre fiction you make a deal with the reader. If you present your book as a mystery, it's going to have a mystery in it, usually a murder. You say you want them to read your romance, they have the right to expect love and a happy ending. Beyond broad genre, reader expectations are built from the title, the cover, the blurb, your past work, excerpts and samples. ... Don't mess with reader expectations.

What I Used to Say & a Slight Update

What I used to say:

If you can do it the other way—by knowing the structure, thinking in high concept sound bites, writing a synopsis first, starting at the beginning and writing the first three chapters—then do it. That's the way the traditional publishing business is designed.

Remember, that is a system designed to benefit the business—not to benefit the creative process.

Have you ever read a book that was a great idea and its first three chapters were dynamite, then it dropped off like a cliff? You can bet that was a terrific proposal and served the business. It did not serve the author's creative process.

The business doesn't care about that, but you should. The creativity is your largest stake in this. It's your value.

Slight update:
As I said, selling on proposal is becoming less common in traditional publishing.

So, it might seem that trad publishers would be less interested in requiring a synopsis well before the book is delivered. Not necessarily so.

They say they use synopses for in-house purposes (cover art, positioning on their list, other rights being picked up by other arms of the company) and marketing.

In addition, more indie authors are marketing well before a book is written through pre-orders and other methods.

Having a compelling synopsis—which is a heck of a lot easier to write if you know the whole story—serves these uses far better than what I often tell my assistant when she's putting up a pre-order. "It's a mystery (or romance or mystery romance or romantic suspense.) I know the body is found wearing a red leather jacket (or some other odd detail.) Then lots of other stuff happens."

So, if you can, I would still say do.

But don't despair if you can't.

We're now leaving the revival meeting portion of this book and entering the important transition (Part III) that will take us to the tools-and-tips-laden Part IV.

PART III

What's in the Survival Kit: The Big Picture

I know some of you skipped right to Part IV. I probably would have, too.

But this next part is really important, so I hope you'll slow down on the rush to the nitty-gritty tools to consider all this … whether it's your first read-through or you're coming back because I put that little reminder at the end of Part IV.

Okay—what's in the Survival Kit that's allowed writers like me to publish, endure, and flourish?

Courage, adventurousness, respect

COURAGE
Learn your process

There is no shortcut here. You just have to write.

Tip: Pay attention to what works well for you and what doesn't.

But without getting hung up in recording or quantifying what worked well and what didn't.

I tend to pay no attention to process during a book. Instead, I look back when it's finished and I'm digging out my office and life from the effects of deadline neglect.

Tip: If you track the number of words or hours you've written in a session, add another column for comments. "Wrote with music." "Left myself notes from yesterday." "Edited yesterday's writing before I started today." "Jumped to next scene I knew." Or whatever you feel influenced your writing for good or ill that day.

Don't track your writing stats? How about making a note any day something felt good or bad about your writing? (No need to do it every day.) Toss the good notes in one box, the bad in another or stick the good Post-Its on one sheet, the bad on another.

Whatever way you've used to gather your observations, at the end of a book, look them over. Look for connecting threads. Pay attention to which ones hit a good or a sour note with you.

On the next book, try more of the good, skip the sour.

See how that works.

Could be you need a bit of the sour to balance things out. Or good and sour shift from book to book.

That last point's important, so don't miss it—each book is an individual experience. You're looking for overall trends, not micro-analyzing.

Keep learning your process, watching for how it alters and grows.

Tip: I recommend assessing after a book is finished because I know a lot of us can get self-conscious about the writing process to the point that analyzing it stops all writing.

Not what we're going for!

If you don't suffer from that and assessing as you go works for you, then terrific.

ADVENTUROUSNESS
Keep honing your process.

Visit the buffet. (Remember, all writing advice is a buffet.) You do not need to pick only one thing or eat what's put in front of you.

Explore the whole buffet. Sure, put some sure-fire winners on your plate, but also experiment, add some of those fruits you've never seen before, take a sample of a salad that sounds bizarre. Try a bite of everything. Hate it? No second bite required. Love it? Go back for more. And remember, what didn't appeal this time, just might next time.

Be active, not passive.

Experiment. For most writers, the writing process is not static. It develops and morphs in small ways and sometimes big ways over time and from project to project. So, there's going to be passive change anyway.

But also deliberately mix in a little change all the time. Keeping things fresh in a more controlled fashion is far better than having your process quit on you out of boredom.

RESPECT
Trust your process.

The experimenting I just recommended comes from a spirit of adventure and keeping things fresh. Not from fear. It's not that your process isn't good enough, it's that it can always be a little better. In other words, don't let This-is-the-only-way types push you into a total revamp.

I was driving back from a weekend conference with a friend years and years ago. One of the workshops had been by a very persuasive and decisive published author who had devised a process that involved color-coded index cards. This workshop was a huge hit. Attendees said this was just what they'd needed to make everything easier. The author giving the workshop promised it would, as long as they followed her directions precisely.

I was lamenting to my friend that my heart had dropped lower and lower and lower during the workshop until now, driving home, I was in despair.

"I can't do it," I told my friend. "Color code every scene for POV, emotion, plot development? I can't. I can feel myself sinking into a color-coded coma that I'd never recover from. But that's the system and it clearly works. I can't do it, so I can't write."

My friend said something I'll never forget:

"Pat, you're an idiot."

Not quite a slap across the face, but it did catch my attention.

She continued, "You've published three books and are under contract for two more. You can't say you can't, because you are doing it."

Oh.

Right.

Yet, I'd been so caught up in the color-coded index card fervor that I had forgotten what my process had already done for me.

I was not respecting my process.

Part of respecting—and valuing—your process is protecting it. Don't let it be dismissed by others, including those who probably believe that they would be doing you a great favor if only you'd listen to them about how to write.

Unless they're inside your head and your creativity, they can't know what's best for your process.

You're the one on that teeter-totter, the one who feels the balance point between respecting, valuing, and protecting your process and the possibility of beneficial learning by experimenting.

Now, you know you're not alone and you're respecting (while honing) your process. Next, in Part IV, specific tools and tips to help you survive.

PART IV

Filling Your Survival Kit

These tools and tips I'm sharing with you—or whatever hints, methods, tricks you cull from other writers or come up with on your own—are vital to writers who don't outline, pre-write, or any of the other think-before-you-write methods, because we don't have as many supporting elements to fall back on.

No color-coded anything, remember? Also no outline or character chart or plot-point map.

Why would we need things to fall back on?

Because most writers get stuck at some point.

And all writers need to stop writing at times to eat, sleep, go to the bathroom, interact with real human beings (if for no other reason than to gather more character traits), take the dog out, and every two years watch the Olympics obsessively (or is that just me?)

So, we also need ways to help us get started again.

Outliners can look at their outline and say, "Oh, yeah, I was at exactly this point. According to my outline, this comes next." Writers who don't write right need other tricks and tools.

Okay, let's hit the actual tools. Starting with the worst news first.

Plotting

If you read the part where pantsers are tagged as overwhelmingly discovery writers, it makes perfect sense that most of us aren't that fond of plotting. Plotting is structure. Pantsing is all the fun, magical bits.

So, brace yourself.

Your book must have structure. That's the bad news.

The good news is **it doesn't need to have structure before you start writing**.

I did a workshop with talented and prolific author Emilie Richards called Writing From the Inside Out and the Outside In. Emilie was the Outside In—structure in to the heart of the characters. I was the Inside Out—the heart of the characters out to structure.

In the end, you must have both structure and the heart of your characters in your novel, but you can get there either way.

(You should have seen our preparation for the presentation—Emilie's talk all neatly typed out word for word, mine on note cards with last-minute addendums, deletions, and arrows to connect my points in a different way. The physical manifestation of our different approaches. But both worked, according to the attendees.)

How does a pantser get to structure?

Very carefully. Da-dum-dum.

As I said in Part I and will detail more, my process is to write what I know when I know it. That means popping out scenes or smaller pieces as they come to me.

Tool: At the beginning, these writings go into one of two files—a main story file in roughly chronological order or a file for not-yet-assigned pieces. The main file is the working name of the story. The second file is the working name and "Move Around."

Tip: Be cautious about what you place in the main file.

I try to restrict this file to the pieces I'm pretty darned sure will go in the order taking shape there. The pieces don't always end up precisely where first placed, and that's fine, but the majority of them do.

If you're like me, it works best when you don't try to assign a chunk of writing before its time. I do better with a sparer spine in this main file than I do with it clogged up with misplaced pieces. That's because of a tendency to make the darned thing work where it was placed, by gum.

Holding off giving it a firm place in the spine of the story allows more time for the right place to reveal itself.

Tip: The second file, the one called "Move Around," groups pieces under oh-so-original headings of "Beginning," "Middle," "End," "Don't Know Yet," and "Lines."

Often there's a sense of which of the big three—Beginning, Middle, End—a chunk belongs in, but with "Don't Know Yet" there's also a spot for the others.

"Lines" is just that. Lines the muse whispered that don't yet have a home.

Keep writing and depositing what's written into these two files until you've run out of steam. That the first part—and most fun—of my process.

What Comes to Me and How

Notice that I did not mention chapters.

I don't recall an entire chapter ever coming to me. So how does this stuff come?

After I've written it (rarely before), I can usually classify the output from writing what I knew as:

- A scene (not often the whole thing comes).
- Part of a scene with lots of notes to myself of what else needs to be included/decided.
- Elements of a theme or thread (often several written together).
- Layers.
- Miscellaneous chunks.

Scenes and Parts of Scenes

The first thing that came to me in what became my first published book, a romance titled **Hoops**, was a scene that ended up in the middle of the book.

I heard and saw a man and a woman talking/arguing on a basketball court. I wrote as fast as I could to keep up with them. By the end of that scene I had a sense of their conflict, though I didn't know their names or a lot of other things about them.

I also had the beginning of another scene between them that came before this scene on the basketball court.

That happens a lot.

In writing one scene that's come to me, pieces of what must have happened earlier and could/should happen later also show up. I don't let those pieces get away.

To indicate I'm out of the main scene, I'll use [later or [earlier and keep going with what's coming to me.

When that out-of-sequence bit tails off (no more words coming), I close with a bracket and a line of space and return to the main scene.

If the bracketed part is a short bit I'll leave it there until I'm ready to deal with that element.

If it's a longer piece I might break it out right then and move it to one of my main files. (See **Moving Around** section.)

Tool: Brackets can be your friend.
I use them to set off notes to myself, or things I need to check—[Chk—or run past a specific person who's a source—[Ask—or the Earlier/Later sections that pop up.

I use brackets because they are easy to type and they do not naturally occur in fiction. That makes them distinct and thus easy to search for.

I also use [To Here to get back to wherever my previous writing session left off. I don't always return the next day to the same place (if a binge is coming on, I'm following it). So this makes it easier to find areas left unfinished.

If you like something other than brackets, go for it. But remember the criteria of not occurring in fiction, easy to type, easy to search.

Elements of a Theme or Thread

Themes and threads are going to end up spread throughout the book, say in four or five steps. But sometimes several or all (lucky you!) of the steps come to you at once.

Tip: Write them when they come to you.

I had one of those in **The Christmas Princess**. How the two main characters interacted going in and out of doors reflected changes in their relationship. Did he distrust her? Was he protecting her? Was she standing up for herself? Were they a team? Those and more questions were acted out at a doorway.

Early in the writing, I wrote the core of all those interactions at one time, showing the pattern/growth across them all. It was easier for me to show the changes—subtly but strongly—because I wrote the interactions all together.

Then I set them aside and later worked each one into a scene that was doing a lot of other work already.

Layers

To me, these are smaller and/or more subtle than the themes or threads. They often don't directly involve or reflect growth or change, yet they can add texture and depth.

These, too, will pop up unexpectedly as I'm writing something else, then need to be dropped in before/after wherever the first one occurred.

For example, in **Wyoming Wildflowers: The Beginning**, the lead characters go back and forth about their favorite holiday songs, cookies, traditions, etc. I liked it the first time they did it, so I made it a recurring topic for them. It carries subtext, especially about the conflict, but not major growth or change.

Tip: Watch for potential themes, threads, and layers if you do periodic readbacks of your WIP (work in progress) and during your early edits. Your subconscious often leaves you these as a gift. It's your job to take the one your subconscious gave you, develop it, and drop variations in additional spots.

Bonus Tip: Use the Rule of Three to your advantage. Make sure you have at least three touches of themes, threads, and layers. The human brain likes patterns and three is the smallest number to consider a pattern.

Make your readers' brains happy!

Miscellaneous Chunks

No idea what else they fit with. No idea where they came from. But there they are.

They are valuable. Do not let them disappear on you. Write them down.

Watch for further developments.

Put them in "Don't Know Yet" until you see where they can serve your story.

Retroactive Plotting

After a while the muse (or writer) runs out of steam. The chunks, layers, themes, scenes, and threads stop coming. Darn it.

Now it's time to dig in.

Tool: This is when I do what I call **Retroactive Plotting**. (What follows is a brief explanation. I do a workshop on this, too … to the complete befuddlement of Plotting/Organized types.)

I look at the scenes/chunks/pieces I have already written and I compare them against my interpretation of the classic **Three-Act Structure**:

Act One
> Set-up
> Other Action Establishing Characters
> First Turning Point—Story Question
> > Raised

Act Two
> Characters Changing—Motivated,
> > Incremental, Believable
> Subplots
> Second Turning Point—Story Question
> > Raised Again
> Black Moment—Looks Like Story
> > Question Answer Will Be Negative

Act Three
> Remaining Subplots Wrapped Up
> Characters' Growth Demonstrated
> Potential Impact of Black Moment
> Climax—Story Question Answer
> Resolution

First, I find where my already-written collection from the main file and the moving around file have hit the necessary structure points (yay!) and where structure is lacking (work ahead).

Say, a scene that could be the First Turning Point is rather light right now. See if it can be beefed up to carry the structure without losing the flavor of the scene.

Or, you might spot that you'd introduced a subplot in Act Two that has no resolution yet. Oops. Need to get that hanging thread woven back in.

Or, you've missed a step in a major character's development/arc and need to add that while also serving a subplot.

This is also the point where I first move pieces around—to help fill the needs of structure, to fulfill character development, to establish a reasonable timeline. (See **Moving Around** section. See **Timeline** section.)

Now's the time to push through the final mists to fill in the gaps. (See **Guilt** section.)

Moving Around

A few pointers if you're moving around pieces, particularly in MS Word, but these can also apply elsewhere.

Tip: Create new files of both your main file and your Moving Around file before starting a moving session. Label them appropriately.

I add the date to the new file and it becomes the active file until the next moving around session.

Tip: Every time you move a piece, save both the file where it came from and the file it's gone to. My house was hit by lightning, it fried my printer, keyboard, monitor, and started a fire on the living room floor, but it didn't fry the hard drive and I lost only about one minute's worth of work during a massive move-around session because I'd done this frequent saving.

Tip: If you've cut a piece to move it and you start to get distracted, go back and undo the cut. That way it's still in its original spot when your distraction lets you get back to it, without the danger of overwriting it by saving something else to Clipboard. If I think it's going to be a short distraction, I park the piece in a new document temporarily.

Tip: Undo can get you back to restore a cut piece (if you haven't yet hit save) but beware the strong potential for having copies of pieces in both files, which can become confusing.

Finding Stuff

Finding the spot in the main file where you want to put a chunk from the move-around file can raise frustrations.

When I started, I would search for phrases or words particular to the main file scene I wanted to add the chunk to. Even with a pretty good memory for what I've written, this was not reliable. I'd be stunned by how many times I'd written "rotten bananas" in a manuscript and would need to sort through them to find the right one. Or it would turn out the scene I wanted actually had the phrase "rotting bananas."

I use wildcards in searches, but found the hunting cumbersome.

With my low frustration threshold, a new method was needed.

Tool: I start every scene/piece/chunk/what-ever with "CHAPTER —" then add a short reminder of what's in the scene. For example, "CHAPTER—Gracie finds body" or "CHAPTER—Sheila at Bunco."

Chunks labeled this way don't always end up as new chapters in the final version of the manuscript. That's fine. This is to identify them for my purposes. You could use GORK if you want. Just select something that won't occur much in your text.

During a move-around session, I do Find for "CHAPTER —" and to pull all those up (and nothing else) in the left margin of the main file and the "Move Around" file.

I see the present order, can easily find pieces I want to move and can easily find target spots for the pieces moving in from the "Move Around" file.

Tip: I also add "Chapter —" before "Beginning," "Middle," "End" to include those categories on the left margin string and quickly see where the piece is coming from.

(I know Scrivener devotees say it can do the same/similar, so if you use Scrivener, check it out.)

Tip: If the order is really being a pain for me, I'll break it down more and do the moving around for Beginning/Middle/End one at a time. I find that helps for longer/more complex stories.

Tip: Plan on multiple move-around sessions—remember, don't force a piece into the chronology. Don't expect to clear out any of the sections, especially the "Don't Know Yet" file, in one pass. You'll need to discover more of the story before that happens.

Tip: As I'm discovering the story, I add a new section to my move around file: "Maybe Not." Sometimes pieces just don't work in this story. I park chunks there until I know for sure. Sometimes they'll migrate to later books. Sometimes they're cut loose.

Tip: If you're moving pieces around, don't bother with finalizing transitions. Do those later, when you're sure/pretty sure the pieces will remain in that spot, so your bridge from one scene/chapter to the next works. Also, knowing what happened in the previous scene makes it so much easier to write a transition. Well, identifies what needs to be in that transition, anyway. The writing is up to you.

Finding Your Own Structure

This path to structure, this way of writing from the inside out, is what works for me, found through trial and error, cobbling together bits and pieces from various writing methods, and held together by my own process.

I'd read innumerable books and gone to gobs of workshops on structure or plotting—the W, the rising action, the hero's journey, the pyramid, the Fichtean Curve (I kid you not), and on and on, hoping each time that this was the answer. None of them was.

For me.

But any of those might be the basis for you to find a path to structure that works for you.

What you're looking for is something that clicks—that makes you say, Oh, now I get it.

When three-act structure clicked for me, I was reading *Making a Good Script Great* by script consultant Linda Seger. I highly recommend it for anyone who plots retroactively, not least because it's presented from the premise that you've already written a bunch on a story and now you're trying to improve it. Its use of familiar movies as illustrations and case studies helped me connect with rhythms I recognized, but hadn't always incorporated into my writing.

I also recommend her other screenwriting books, as well as Syd Field's *Screenplay*.

Another to try is Michael Hauge's *Writing Screenplays That Sell*, focusing on Part One, and his Story Mastery Workshop, if it comes to a conference near you.

Christopher Vogler's Hero's Journey concept resonates with many, many authors. He and Hauge now have an audiobook called *The Hero's 2 Journeys* that presents some of each of their views.

But, truly, this is a journey you're going to need to take on your own.

The Structure-Seeker's Journey

Tip: Note that a lot of these recommended sources are aimed at screenplays. That's no accident. Structure's skeleton is generally more visible in a screenplay. Many screenplay approaches readily adapt to novel-writing.

Tip: I'm a big proponent of buying books to support authors, but holy moly, you can run through a lot of royalties paying for expensive structure books that don't click for you. I recommend trying them out through your library first.

When you find the ones that work for you, invest in them.

I'm on my fourth copy of *Making a Good Script Great* and have probably sold a thousand copies of it through recommendations in workshops and classes I've taught.

Tool: Test out the theory of a proposed structure against a story/movie you know really, really well. I can do my Retroactive Plotting using *A Christmas Carol* (1938 version or the Muppets) in my sleep.

Tool: Then test it against a story/movie you're watching for the first or second time. Can you still find the structure's markers when you aren't as familiar with the happenings of the story? Because you need something that's not so esoteric to you that you have to go digging for it. You want it to smack you in the face. Remember: Oh, now I get it.

Tool: Test it on something you've written and completed. Does it add value to your work? Are you already doing some/much of what it recommends, but it can help you make your work stronger? In my opinion, that's ideal. You've already internalized some of it because it makes sense to you down in your story-consuming bones. You just needed a boost to a stronger structure.

Tip: I would think very carefully before using anything that entailed a complete revamp of your approach to story. I'm not ruling it out completely, but be sure it's not just another way to feel like you're advancing your writing when you're not. There's cleaning a closet, then there's taking an architecture course to build the perfect closet (with a house attached) from scratch … while never cleaning the closet. **Cough** Online solitaire. **Cough**

Tool: Only after the other steps are completed do you consider applying a new-to-you structure to your WIP (work in progress.).

Tip: Remember the buffet! You do not need to swallow any method whole. Look for the parts that work for you.

Tip: Do not despair. There's something out there that will work for you.

If there's interest, I might put together a book on Retroactive Plotting. So, let me know if you'd like that. If not, no worries, because that will leave me more time for writing fiction. ;-)

Brainstorming

The useful and powerful tool of brainstorming is not limited to those of us who don't write right, but it might be even more vital for us than the plotters.

When we stall on a story, it's most often during the raw, emotional stage of writing, rather than the more analytical stage of structure/outlining. The stall can feel like a permanent state.

If you hit a stall or wall or block or whatever you call it, you won't be surprised that my first recommendation is to jump to writing something you know.

But sometimes that won't work. Say, you have to make a decision about what exactly happened in a character's childhood that's making him act the way he's acting, because several plot points hinge on it and those are the scenes left to write so you can't move on without deciding.

Step into the brainstorm.

Tip: To brainstorm with others or not? Tricky question. Over the many years of doing this, I've found it was more often than not dangerous to brainstorm big picture or general ideas with anyone else.

Too frequently, the recommendations of others took me away from the sensed-but-not-yet-articulated (even internally) feel of the story. Too many mists remained for others to understand what I felt about the story.

I had far better success by brainstorming with fellow writers on a specific aspect of a character who was giving me trouble in a story that had already gelled in my head.

In other words, probably after the point where I'd run out of steam writing what I knew.

Because then the other suggestions don't disrupt that delicate balance I've found as I work through the mists.

In one instance from years ago, three other authors latched onto what I'd told them and the question I was wrestling with and dismissed everything I'd so far seen through the mists—and I do mean everything.

Instead, they told me it should be an entirely different story. It was like someone turning on jet-propelled fans to rip through the mists, while simultaneously transforming the horizon I'd partially glimpsed from a gently rolling land-scape into a high-rise city center.

When I tried to stop them, I was told I was wrong and I needed to toughen up.

These people almost certainly thought they were doing me a favor.

They did teach me a lesson.

To be far more careful about what—and when—I told people about my stories.

You will need to find the too-soon point for yourself. But I recommend erring on the side of caution until you've plotted (in the surveyor sense, rather than the writer sense) those bounda-ries.

More about brainstorming, whether by your-self or with others:

Tip: Ask a specific question: "How else can I show his poverty-stricken childhood?" "What happened to him in his previous relationship that is causing X behavior?"

Tip: Require yourself to write at least 25-30 answers as fast as you can. That's the absolute minimum. I find 50 answers is much better.

Tip: Figure 15 answers per 10 minutes. If that seems easy, allow less time.

Tip: Set a timer.

Tip: No stopping until the timer goes off.

Tip: No judging.

Tip: Recognize that the purpose of the first 20 or so answers is to blow out the cobwebs, so expect the tried, true, and trite.

Tip: Recognize that toward the end desperation sets in and you'll get some bizarre stuff. Aliens show up a lot in my last few answers.

Tip: Recognize that one or two workable ideas is a bonanza in a list of 50.

Tip: No workable ideas? Do it again. Immediately. No repeating ideas.

Tip: If you do it with a writing pal brainstorming for you simultaneously, pay close attention to the ideas that are not trite and don't involve aliens (unless you're writing science fiction), yet show up on both your lists.

Tip: An alternative form of brainstorming is calling a writer pal and having them let you pour out what the issue is. Frequently, this will bring you the answer without them saying a word. For unknown reasons this does not work without an audience.

I've wandered around the house explaining the issue to myself, the dog, the furniture, and non-writer civilians, and none of that helps. It has to be a fellow writer. The phone seems to help. And long distance is a bonus. I bet overseas would be even better.

Don't ask me to explain.

Characters

People and their dialogue are what come to me most easily in stories, so I have the fewest tricks here.

The major point is that major characters must change over the course of the book. That change needs to be motivated, incremental, and believable. Yup, that's another whole workshop and far too broad and fundamental to fit into the toolkit.

But here are a couple pieces of advice:

Tool: If a character has gone off the rails, go back and check who s/he was at the beginning of the story and who s/he becomes by the end of the story.

- Check if you're trying to jump them too far too fast in the process.
- Check if there's no reason for the way they're changing.
- Check if the change is heading the wrong direction.

Tool: If characters are being recalcitrant about revealing themselves, talk to them.

Actually, arguing with and/or griping at them works best. Preferably while you're doing something else—digging in the garden, vacuuming, doing laundry. (Truly, doing this while doing something else helps. I figure it distracts your mind just enough to let the character's thoughts flow.)

Jibes work well. "Yeah, you'd probably tell me this wasn't the time of year to transplant hostas. You're so anal." … "Because it works better when you do things in the proper season. There is a season to everything." … "Oh, brother, where'd you come up with that one?" … "My grandmother, who was a missionary." … "Say what? Uh, tell me about her."

Ask them a question: "Who are you?" might work for a minor character, but more specific is better. "Why is that red leather jacket so important to you?"

I once asked a character, "Why are you reacting xyz way in this scene?" And he argued that it wasn't "xyz" way it was "efg" way. In other words, he didn't like my word choice in characterizing how he was reacting. When I looked at it from the angle of his alternative word choice, bingo!

It's important to say that this is not a character interview, where you write down favorite color, high school mascot, and other details. You are starting arguments/asking questions to get to specific—generally emotional—information and having it come in the character's voice.

Nor is this an exercise. I'd say that over the years I've used seventy to eighty percent of the responses that have come from this. One example was in my romance, **The Unexpected Wedding Guest**. I knew something major happened to the heroine, Suz, in the past, but not what. So, I ask her, "Why do you feel this way?" And just started writing.

The stuff that came at the beginning was true and real and part of her background, but not germane to the story and wasn't used. But after about four paragraphs, the good stuff started coming.

What About Character Charts?

They sound so useful, don't they? How could it possibly hurt to know all this stuff about your character? Favorite childhood game, most hated subject in school, best memory of the Fourth of July, and on and on.

Be very careful. Charts, like character interviews, can be procrastination. It seems like you're working. To an outsider it might look like you're working. But all too often filling out these charts is really just another form of—you guessed it—online solitaire.

Organizing as You Go

For me, organizing needs to follow the writing, rather than try to lead it.

I create a few files, then fill them in as I write, not beforehand.

Two of these organizing elements I do for every book and an additional two for some books.

Organizing Files for Every Book

Cast list:
- First and last names of every character (always). This is to avoid having Robin Roberts and Robert Robin in the same story.
- Role in the book/job (frequently). This might be "prime suspect's girlfriend" in a mystery or "neighboring rancher" in a romance.

- Relationships to other characters (sometimes). Mostly when I'm starting a new series and sorting out the people.
- Traits, foibles, physical stuff (depends). Which side the limp's on, eye/hair color. In mysteries there might be more—kind of vehicle, handedness, other aspects that might be clues or red herrings.

I always keep it short. These are not for character creation. They are quick memory reminders for subsequent mentions of a character already created.

Timeline:
In the early stages of writing, I put [Timeline] in a scene to insert a time/day reference later. If the scene is showing up on the screen as happening at night or needs to be on a Saturday because the farmer's market is busiest then, I'll note that.

After my first draft has a beginning, middle, and end, and a lot of the scenes are written or identified as needing to be written, I will either write out a list of days/dates and times or print out multiple copies of a blank grid to use for a calendar.

In Word, I do a search for "[Timeline" and all instances—including those with "night" or "Saturday" or whatever else I've added—will pop up on the left-hand side.

I'll use those to draft the timeline first, then pin down details and make a good copy … which usually gets changed around again later.

The timeline is fluid until my final edit(s). For example, I've condensed timelines during very late drafts to improve pacing.

Organizing Files for Some Books
(Usually ones giving me problems)

Plot points:

My usual process of checking in with the three-act structure is in my head. But if something's not gelling, I will write out the structure. This can be on scrap paper, legal pad, or in the computer.

I jot down the "Chapter —" identifier for a scene next to the elements of the three-act structure.

Don't get fancy with this. Like charts, it can become another version of online solitaire. Do just enough to see the shape of the story.

Tip: My most frequent issue is trying to make a scene carry a major structure element that it's not meant to carry. Often this requires writing an additional scene to do that work, and my muse was trying to get away with a shortcut.

Or maybe it was me. But I'm betting on the muse.

Character arcs:
This is to check that the character arcs—for main characters and any secondary characters who change significantly—have hit the necessary points to make that change incremental, motivated, and believable.

I'll check and jot down (nothing formal) the elements that satisfy the needs of that character arc … looking for what's missing so I can fix it.

Binging vs. Chipping Away

My writer pal Gina Wilkins describes both of us as binge and purge writers. She's right, but I like to pretty it up by thinking of my two modes of writing as Binging and Chipping Away.

Writing what I know, when I know it is binge writing. It comes without my knowing where it's heading or where it came from.

Then there's chipping away writing.

This is the harder part for me.

This is conscious, deliberate, word-by-word writing. It is filling in all the things I know need to be in the story—plot points, missing elements, completing scenes, transitions, additional layers, an errant step in a thread—but that didn't come winging into my head and out to the computer. Darn it.

Binge writing is whipping along with the top down and a blue sky overhead. Chipping away is driving in rush hour traffic in a downpour.

But it must be done.

Tip: This is where I focus on BicHoking— that's Butt in Chair, Hands on Keyboard.

Have you BicHoked today?

There is no substitute for it.

Ways to Get Yourself to Write

No need to worry about this when the words are pouring out. That's the magic time of writing. When someone holding a mega check ringing your doorbell makes you say Leave. Me. Alone.

But then there are the other times.

When the magic stops and you have 50k words of a projected 90k book left to write. When you cannot resist the basement's siren song of

"Clean me. Clean me now." Because surely that would be more fun.

How do you get yourself to BicHok then?

It's very simple. Not easy, but simple. It boils down to mind games, with a side of guilt.

Mind Games

Tool: Visit the story daily.
The idea is to keep it fresh in your mind. Even if you only do a few hundred words, it brings it from the back to the front of your subconscious, it keeps the heat on under the burner as ideas simmer.

Plus, you have a few more hundred words than you would have otherwise.

Tool: Leave yourself notes at the end of each writing session.
For me, this is a mind dump of what I'm thinking about, snatches of dialogue or description or how this scene connects to others. These fragments are separated by … or sometimes [.

When I start my next writing session, I start with those notes, filling in each … to form complete sentences, paragraphs, passages.

That filling in process brings my mind back to where it was during the previous session.

It's also a warmup and stretching period. By the time the notes are filled in, I'm on my way.

Some edit what they wrote the previous session with the same goal. If you write in sequence, that might work for you. If you're an out-of-sequence writer it's not as useful.

Tool: Beware chapter endings.

Even if you don't use the notes-at-the-end-of-a-session tool, be very, very wary of ending a session at the end of a chapter. It's a wrap-up, an incremental completion that your brain interprets as "Done! Let's go have fun" and that thought sinks in deeper and deeper until you sit down at the computer again and your brain says, "What the heck? We were done. What's this about more work?"

Ending a writing session with the end of a chapter is the Friday night of your writing life and it makes the next writing session such a Monday morning. Don't do that to yourself.

Tool: Write down three things you'd like to write in your next session.

While the notes to yourself are breadcrumbs that lead you back into the world of the story where you left it, these three are lavishly iced cupcakes—treats all the way.

Mentally revisit these before you go to sleep, when you wake up. If you don't get to some of your treat ideas in your next writing session, you can recycle them the next day. But if today's session leaves you with three different things that are more exciting to write tomorrow, then go with those over the not-yet-dones.

You can use them another day if you need to fill in your list of three.

Or you'll get to them at the end of the book. (See **Guilt** section.)

Or you'll discover they're not needed after all.

My notes on what I want to do the next session are rarely long or complex. Might be "work in Clara's line about LuLu" or "add to thread about leather jacket" or "what Elizabeth thinks about Fine's tantrum."

They're more often tidbits than entire scenes. Their purpose is to jazz me up to come back to the writing.

Tool: Skip to what you know.

You knew this one was coming, right?

It's there in your head. Pieces of a scene. Full-blown, Technicolor, and every nuance of dialogue.

But it's not until just before the Black Moment.

Write it.

Write it now.

It will come far faster than trying to slog your way up to it with scenes that must be written but don't thrill you.

It will jazz you up about writing. The sort of writing session that makes you dance around afterward and sing. Never a bad thing.

It will be there, in one of your two files, reminding you that its beauty and splendor will be for naught if you don't write all the other scenes around it. (See **Guilt** section.)

Tip: There's a ninety-percent chance that writing this scene will reveal things you didn't know about other scenes or the story as a whole. Gather those gifts from the muse while you may.

There's a forty-percent chance that this scene will part the mists from another (or multiple other) scenes.

Tool: Write what you're excited about writing.

Most of the benefits of writing what you know also apply to writing what you're excited about. Go back up and reread them to check.

Especially the one about jazzing you up about writing.

Stringing together writing what you know and what you're excited about writing can get you so deep into a book that it's natural for guilt to pull you the rest of the way. (See **Guilt** section.)

Tool: Write what you're most afraid of writing.

This sounds contradictory to the previous tools, but it works. It seems to free up the muse, opening more "know" and "excited to write" bursts. Perhaps they can't get out past your fear. So, you must remove that block by plunging right into it.

Important Tip: This chunk does not need to be perfect or even good to achieve this benefit. You need to get something down on paper/screen.

Do not get caught up with revising or editing it. You can fix it later, once the other parts of the story are done and you can see clearly what needs to be done with it.

Tell yourself you can throw it out.

Tell yourself it's an adventure.

Tell yourself it's a Survivor episode for your muse.

Tool: Read/Watch in chunks.

Having trouble with a scene? Say, a first kiss in romance, intro of the villain in a thriller, the finding of the body in a mystery.

Grab a stack of books or a folder in your digital library. Read 15-20-30 first-kiss/villain-intro/body-find/whatever's bogging you down scenes. Don't get sidetracked into reading anything else of those books, just those scenes.

Read in other genres if they offer similar scenes. Toss in movies. Maybe try some music, searching for the "sound" of your scene.

Read/consume fast. You're not analyzing, you're not looking for technique, and you're absolutely, positively, not **ever** looking for details to use in your work.

Not a Tip. A Commandment: Do. Not. Copy. **Ever**.

It's stealing.

Those with no ethics who might be okay with that, would still be idiots. They'd get an inferior Frankenbook. The reason a scene—or even a phrase—works so wonderfully in a book is because of all that came before it. It's an integral part of that book. Not someone else's. It will sound off anywhere other than its natural habitat.

Besides, **It. Is. Stealing**.

So, why am I recommending gobbling up scenes covering similar territory to the one you're stuck on?

To connect with the feel of those numerous scenes.

By connecting with those various feels, you will start recognizing the emotions that need to come across in your scene. Once you have the emotions, the dialogue, the actions, then the flow of the scene will follow.

When I do this, I start getting a squirmy, itchy feeling as I'm gobbling these other scenes. No, no, no. Nothing's harmonizing with my scene's needs, nothing's resonating, nothing's triggering ideas for my story.

That's okay. This is not wasted time.

Knowing what isn't right will help you discover what is right. Keep going.

Find that one thread. Then play with it. The smallest thread can lead you to the heart of your scene.

You read a scene that says the kiss was as light as cotton candy. Cotton candy—sweet. No. Totally wrong. She'd be tart—lemon.

And then you have a line—She tasted of lemonade. Cool, bright, and tart.

Now play off that line. How does she have him thinking of lemonade in northern Minnesota in January? Are there other associations or interactions from your story that can highlight that? Has she griped about the cold weather? But now he finds she brings summer with her.

Does lemonade or tartness or the contrast of lemonade/winter connect to other elements in the book? How can you connect it? How does feeling she brings summer with her interact with his emotions? How does it make him react? Pull away? Go for more kissing despite his better judgment? Mutter something that makes sense to him, but won't to her until the end.

Work it!

And keep going with more books/movies/music gobbling. You want multiple possible threads so you can weave the best in and let the others go.

Tool: Do that chipping away writing.

It has to be done. You're sitting there in front of the computer. Might as well knock off some of the necessities.

BicHoking is honorable work.

Ahh, but if a binge starts, go with it!

Tool: Trade off with a second project.

Let the first one build up steam in your subconscious while you roll out what's there at the surface on the second one, then go back to the first one.

That can mean alternating days or working on one for several days before taking a break with another or writing on both the same day.

I often work on two (or more) projects simultaneously early in the process, writing on both the same day. When I've depleted what I know about the first one for that day, I jump to the second. I rarely write as much on the B story on any day, but some is better than none.

I can't do this once I reach the move-around stage. I need all my writing brain space for one story at that point.

Experiment to see if it works for you and when in your process it works best for you.

Tool: Deadlines.

Deadlines make me let go.

Deadlines make me make hard choices.

They make me let go of the illusion of perfection, of the illusion that I can jam everything possible into this one story.

At the beginning, a story can be anything and everything. But to tell a story other people can follow, you must eliminate some of the possibilities.

I resist this difficult truth mightily unless forced to face it by a deadline.

For me, these must be external deadlines. Self-deadlines established because they would make my life easier/saner? Pffft. Forget them.

But if I've promised an editor or the readers (via pre-order or an announced date in my newsletter), then I'm bound to it.

Fear of deadline is a powerful, powerful motivator for this long-time journalist. (Did I learn the power of deadlines from journalism or was I drawn to journalism because I needed deadlines? The mystery remains...)

Talk about peer pressure, try failing to get your story in on time so there's no coverage of that event for the readers. Or try missing a deadline as an editor, which means the edition goes out without new stories written by coworkers.

Internalize that gut punch.

Know that the first half of that word is not kidding.

Dead.

Then do what you have to do to meet that deadline.

In mid-2018 I missed my first deadline in about 50 books. (I know, I should go back and count those, too, along with the USA Today spots.)

I pushed a pre-order back by 12 days.

Everyone said it wasn't a huge delay. I had good reasons and don't at all regret allocating my time to those other reasons. Readers were wonderfully supportive.

Still, I felt awful.

Just awful.

I told a family member it had been a point of honor with me to never miss a deadline.

My dear, sympathetic family member replied, "So now you have no point and no honor."

(Anybody want a family member? I'll sell you this one. Cheap.)

But it was true, darn it.

So, remember that if you consider breaking a deadline—no point, no honor.

And get back to writing.

Tool: Accountability.
Break your project down into smaller pieces and pledge to reach certain benchmarks by certain dates or times.

If you're terrifically self-motivated, that accountability can be to yourself. (Never works for me, alas.)

Go up a notch with written accountability through a checklist, calendar, or countdown software that dings at you.

Tip: What works best for most writers is to be accountable to other people (actually to yourself via other people).

Join or create a group, then set your goals, pledge to meet them, and require updates of how each of you is doing.

I think it's important to set your own goals, rather than blanket goals set by the group.

Nudge yourself a little past where you're comfortable, then go for it.

If someone starts slacking off a lot, kick them out of the group unless/until they conform, because they can bring the rest of you down, too.

Oh, see, Horace isn't meeting his goals, why should I?

It's insidious.

The only possible upside to slackers is if you're making your goals and you can boast. That can be a motivation for some. Know yourself.

Tip: I particularly like sprints.

Rather than committing to report your progress for evermore, you set up a specific time period.

I've done them with groups for a few hours, a day, a couple days, a week. NaNoWriMo (National Novel Writing Month) is basically a sprint for the month of November. (A man or a non-Thanksgiving celebrating person must have chosen November, because the only month worse would be December.)

For the longer sprints, I recommend preparing beforehand—pay bills, stock food/meals, have clean clothes ready, move appointments out of this period.

And will somebody please see what they can do about moving NaNoWriMo to a different month?

Tool: Routine.

Honestly, this is a rumor to me. I don't have routines. Especially writing routines. No schedule, no special spot, no sacred sequence before I start.

As I said earlier, I don't want to feel limited about how or where or when I write. (Except I don't do mornings. But that has nothing to do with writing.)

On the laptop on the deck in the afternoon? At the desktop in the evening? Keyboard and iPad mini on an airplane? Phone with a stylus in the Notes app? Dictating into Google Docs while cutting carrots for soup? I do them all. (The phone with a stylus isn't fun, but worked in a pinch on a plane … sounds like a Dr. Seuss title, doesn't it?)

But I know routines work for some people. I also know some how-to writers insist on them. Which might be part of my feeling about them. ;-)

You know what I'm going to say—this is part of the buffet. Try it. See if it works for you. Jiggle it around and see if something else works better.

A couple small routine-ish things I've used.

Tip: Music.

I frequently write to music, especially in the early stuff-is-coming-to-me stage. And I know many other authors do, too.

I can tell you what works best with music for me, but you're going to have to find your own, because I know authors who successfully write to the opposite.

If you listen to my podcast, **Authors Love Readers**, you will have heard many authors talk about whether and how they listen to music. You'll get lots of great ideas there.

For me:

- No lyrics. Because I will start typing what they're singing.

Some non-English songs work for me, but if I know the song too well and it's in French, Spanish, Italian or something else I can pick up, I'll start typing what they're singing. Sometimes in the language they're singing, sometimes in English. Either way, it's not advancing my story.

- Upbeat/energetic classical and movie/TV soundtracks. A particular benefit of sound tracks is their variety of mood and pace.

I find my typing speed matches the tempo of the music.

- A playlist or some other way of playing the music that does not require periodic fiddling with tech, taking my brain out of writing mode. You want your writing session to end before the music does. Or if you're really good, at the same time. ;-)

Streaming works great as long as you've set up the playlist (you don't want anything off-mood to throw you) and you can make it long enough.

I use an old six-DVD player that will cycle back and start again if I go that long in a session. If it's the right mood for what I'm writing, I can repeat a CD with one button and no thinking.

I use the same six CDs throughout a book, sometimes two books. Two to three CDs almost always carry over to the next grouping as well. I like the continuity.

- Keep this music for writing only. If I start doing anything other than writing fiction, I turn it off. You're trying to train yourself into one of Pavlov's dogs. You listen to this particular music when you write. After a while, listening to the music triggers the writing. Wahoo!

Tip: A snow globe.

No kidding. I believe it was Eric Maisel who recommended it at a Novelists, Inc., conference in 2006.

If my brain is particularly fragmented when I sit down to write, I will pick up a tiny snow globe from beside my monitor. It's a streetscape from New Orleans. (I particularly like the idea of snow in New Orleans.) Shake it. Then, as the flakes drift down, I think, those are all my non-writing thoughts drifting down, settling into peace. And quiet.

Tip: A list.

If those non-writing thoughts are to-dos, I write them down. I'll also assign a day/time of day to do them.

Once taken care of in that way, they'll usually leave me alone long enough to get my words in.

GUILT

My theory is it makes good sense to use the natural resources you've got.

I've got guilt. I'm going to use it.

I know, I know, we should all work hard to step away from guilt.

If you've achieved that zen state, then this tool is not for you.

But, if you're like me and guilt is still part of your life, why not make it work for you?

How?

Nag—or "urge yourself on" if you want to spin it—by reminding yourself of a few guilts about not writing:

- You are wasting your gift.

How many people on this planet want to tell stories, but don't know how? You know there are millions of them. You've sat next to them on airplanes, in classes, at meetings, during parties. You've heard them say how much they long to write a book. Someday.

While you *do* have the gift and you're not using it to its fullest at this moment because you're not writing when you should or could be.

You were given the amazing ability to create universes out of twenty-six letters and you're going to go to the mall? Are you nuts?

- You become one of those I'm-going-to-write-a-book-someday people nobody

believes ever will actually write a book
unless you sit down and write today. Now.
- You are disrespecting your muse.

This is more specific than wasting your gift. If
not for your muse, your creativity, or whatever
you want to call it, this story idea you should be
working on would not exist.

It came from somewhere. And it's pretty
darned rude to not give the story the attention it
deserves.

Also, what happens next time? Think you'll
get anymore inspirations from that source when
you haven't held up your end of the bargain?

Nope.

In other words, you're accountable to your
muse, too. Get cracking.

- You are leaving these poor characters in
  bits and pieces strewn all over your
  computer.

This is a powerful one for me, especially because those characters keep yakking in my head.

And what are you going to do about that?
Give them away? You can't. They're yours. More

important, you're theirs. You are their only way to ever come to life and step out into the world.

No one else in the universe can know them as you do, can tell their story.

If you don't sit down and write, they die.

(Hey, I don't mess around with this guilt stuff.)

- Find your individual guilt buttons.

Way back when I bought my first personal computer, I funded it by asking my parents for a short hiatus from payments on their house down payment loan.

They said sure and never bugged me about it. So there was no external accountability about this. It was all guilt.

I strongly felt both their support and the need to repay their generosity. It kept me BicHoking at times I would have preferred to read, take a nap, watch TV, weed the garden, or clean a closet.

My first royalty check finished paying them off in full.

One Last Tool

Editing.

If your "not-right" process resembles mine at all, you're not a one-draft writer. You're likely to have some very rough patches in that rough draft.

It's your obligation—to your story and your reader—to be an exacting editor.

Beyond typos, you are particularly vulnerable to:

Tip: Inconsistencies.

We all do the eye-color changing thing where a character starts with blue eyes and ends up with brown without benefit of color contacts. The **Cast List** helps greatly with this. But edit carefully for it, too.

Tip: Continuity.

Be careful to check that the logic of what your characters are doing and how they are interacting follows from scene to scene. Have your sleuth team angry at each other at the end of one scene, but working together fine in the next? Fix that. Or are they yo-yoing from happy to angry to happy to angry. Fix that, too.

You also must check for things like Wanda referring to another character as dead before the body's turned up. (Unless it's a slip and Wanda's the murderer, of course.)

Moving pieces around means you must edit assiduously for continuity errors.

Tip: Transitions.

Go over them again. Make sure you're drawing the reader from one scene to the next.

Also check that you haven't left a cliffhanger, even a mini one, at the end of a scene or chapter that is never resolved.

Tip: Timeline.

If you move pieces around, you open the gate to having a goof somewhere in the timeline. Go through the close-to-final draft one more time to be sure.

Be sure to be aware of holidays falling within your timeline. You won't want your characters missing the fireworks on the Fourth of July in the U.S.

Tip: Check those plot points and character arcs again.

Especially if you thought they were fine. (If they were troubling you, you probably already checked. It's the ones you think are fine that can bite you in the you-know-where.)

Tip: Overall read.

Go over the whole thing again—see the story, the book as a whole. Try to experience it as a reader would.

But the main thing you have to do is write.

For most of us non-right writers, writing is part of the thinking process. You can think and plan and ask yourself questions forever—but you have to actually write it.

For us, there is something about fingers on the keyboard that unlocks the muse.

After you argue with your characters or ask them a question, don't just run it through your head—Write It.

Here's a truth—Ohhh, maybe even a secret. Possibly the secret, so maybe I under fibbed at the beginning of this:

> You are not going to get your answer and then write it.
>
> You are going to get your answer by writing.
>
> The more you write, the clearer the story will become.

In other words:

Don't wait for clarity to write.
Write your way into focus.

Now, if you haven't read Part II and Part III yet, go back and read them. No demerits. I might have skipped ahead, too, for the nitty-gritty hints of Part IV. But Part II and Part III tackle the broader context that can help you think about your process and how to best use the tips and tools from Part IV.

Maybe my process is similar to yours, maybe not. Maybe you have an entirely different way of writing that's not "right."

Whatever lets you get the words on the page/up on the screen, that's your process. It's both unique and mutable. Nurture it, expand it, hone it, tend it.

Do look for ways to make you process stronger.

Don't waste a moment wondering if you're doing it "right."

Now, go write.

Happy writing!

**Another writers' handbook from
Patricia McLinn**

WORD WATCH

A writer's guide to word usage

Can't get enough on writers and writing?

Listen to the Authors Love Readers podcast, a conversation between host Patricia McLinn and guest novelists about how and why they create the stories their readers love. You can also listen to archived interviews at www.authorslovereaders.com/podcast.

About the author

USA Today bestselling author Patricia McLinn has published more than 50 books, including *Word Watch: A Writer's Guide to the Slippery, Sneaky and Otherwise Tricky.* Her fiction titles include mysteries, romantic suspense, contemporary romance, historical romance and women's fiction. They have topped bestseller lists and won numerous awards.

McLinn learned to read at a tender age as a matter of self-preservation, because older siblings spelled words to keep secrets from her. She wanted to be a novelist from then on, though there was a detour. She received a BA in English Composition from Northwestern University, adding a masters in journalism from Northwestern's Medill School of Journalism in her fourth year.

McLinn became a sportswriter at a time when women doing that were rare, starting at the Rockford (Ill.) Register-Star and becoming assistant sports editor at the Charlotte (N.C.)

Observer before moving on a 20-year career at The Washington Post.

A past president of the independent authors' association Novelists Inc., she has taught writing courses and spoken about writing and the publishing business from Melbourne, Australia, to Washington, D.C., including being a guest speaker at the Smithsonian Institution. She also hosts the Authors Love Readers podcast, inter- viewing authors from a range of fiction genres about how and why they create stories.

Now living in northern Kentucky, McLinn loves to hear from readers through her website and social media.

Also by Patricia McLinn

Fiction/Mystery

Caught Dead in Wyoming series

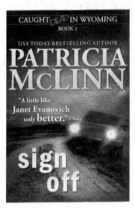

SIGN OFF

Divorce a husband, lose a career … grapple with a murder.

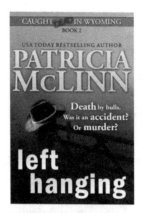

LEFT HANGING

Trampled by rodeo bulls—an accident?

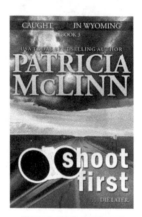

SHOOT FIRST

For Elizabeth, death hits close to home.

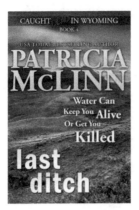

LAST DITCH

A man in a wheelchair goes missing in dangerous country.

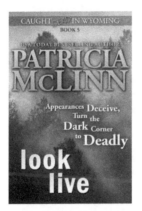

LOOK LIVE

Intriguing out-of-towners help—and hinder— solving a misleading murder.

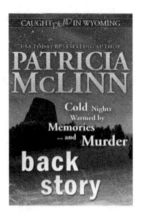

BACK STORY

Murder never dies, but comes back to threaten
Elizabeth and friends.

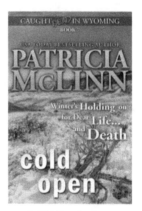

COLD OPEN

Elizabeth's search for a place of her own becomes
an open house for murder.

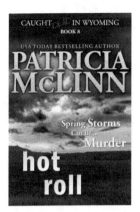

HOT ROLL

Death on a tight deadline for Elizabeth and the team.

Secret Sleuth series

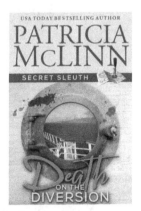

DEATH ON THE DIVERSION

Final resting place? Deck chair.

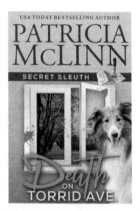

DEATH ON TORRID AVENUE

A new love (canine), an ex-cop and a dog park discovery.

DEATH ON BEGUILING WAY

Sheila untangles a yoga instructor's murder.

Mystery with romance

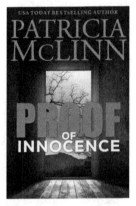

PROOF OF INNOCENCE

She's a prosecutor chasing demons. He's wrestling them.

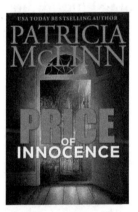

PRICE OF INNOCENCE

She is dedicated to forgiveness. His world is unforgiving.

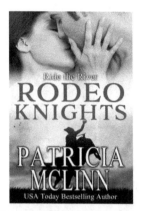

RIDE THE RIVER: RODEO KNIGHTS

Her rodeo cowboy ex is back … as her prime suspect.

Fiction/Romance
Wyoming Wildflowers series

THE BEGINNING

They are worlds apart—can they bridge the distance?

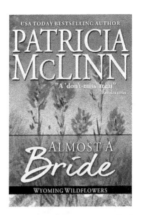

ALMOST A BRIDE

Dave has everything he wants, except the woman he loves.

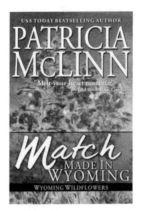

MATCH MADE IN WYOMING

Cal and Taylor can spark a wildfire, but will they burn out?

MY HEART REMEMBERS

Lisa's carried a secret in her heart for years—and he just hit town.

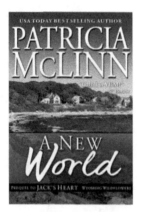

A NEW WORLD

Prequel to Jack's Heart

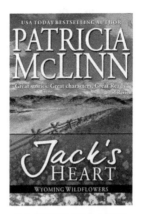

JACK'S HEART

New England single mom meets her Lone Ranger

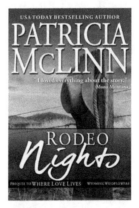

RODEO NIGHTS

Prequel to Where Love Lives

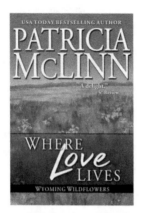

WHERE LOVE LIVES

One night stands in the way of spending the rest of their days together.

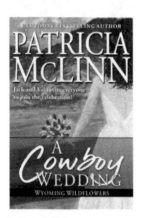

A COWBOY WEDDING

Love is complicated at the Slash-C shindig.

Other romance series

The Wedding Series
Seasons in a Small Town
Marry Me
A Place Called Home
Bardville, Wyoming
Western historicals

Explore all Patricia's books at
www.patriciamclinn.com/patricias-books

Or print a booklist from
www.patriciamclinn.com/patricias-
books/printable-booklist

Buy digital books online directly
from **Patricia's eBookstore** at
www.patriciamclinn.com/patricias-
books/ebookstore

For news about Patricia's upcoming fiction titles, as well as updates from the publishing world, join **Patricia McLinn's Readers List**. You can sign up for her twice-monthly free newsletter here: www.patriciamclinn.com/readers-list

Visit with Patricia:

Website: www.patriciamclinn.com

Facebook: facebook.com/PatriciaMcLinn

Twitter: @PatriciaMcLinn

Pinterest: pinterest.com/patriciamclinn

Instagram: instagram.com/patriciamclinnauthor